WE NEED YOU

A Call to an Imaginal Reality

AMY MCTEAR

Library of Congress Control Number: 2016903638

We Need You: A Call To Imaginal Reality / Amy McTear

p. cm.

ISBN 978-0-9972289-0-8

Photos by Getty Images

Book design by
Holly Moxley of Tracking Wonder Consultancy.

Printed in the United States of America

To my three children, Reilly, Fiona and Kieran,
and to the child within us all who dreams of a better world.
And to my mother and father, Nancy and Tom McTear, who
tirelessly encouraged me to be fully me.

"The greater danger for most of us lies not in setting our aim too high and falling short; but in setting our aim too low, and achieving our mark."

–Michelangelo

part one

The Call

First, let's get clear about why we're not here.

Though we are here to get along, we are not here to go along.

We are not here to blend in or disappear or to make decisions based on fear.

We are not here to be invisible or miserable, inaudible or unseen, cogs in someone else's machine - whether corporate, cultural or anything in between.

We are not here to live shallow, to swallow our voice, or to believe following what matters to us most is not a choice.

We did not come to live almost, to sing someone else's song, or to take someone else's ride by suppressing the dreamer inside.

We are not here to be careless, destructive, or needy, to prolong suffering, increase the ranks of the greedy.

We're not here to stand alone, nor here to be chained, powerless, apathetic, unable to change.

We are here on a mission.

We are here on duty.

We are here for mastery, excellence, & beauty.

We are here to heal from our temporary amnesia

& remember our purpose as human beings,

to assume our role in the universe's great "one turning."

We are here to take chances and claim what matters,

to let inner vision inform decision,

to fail, begin again, and revision.

We are here to free the dreamer inside,

to thrive, to rise, collaborate, cooperate, and actualize.

We are here to fill our own shoes,

create the world we would choose,

"let the beauty we love be what we do"

And we need you.

part two

Our Dispirited
Dream

"THE WORLD JUST SEEMS all wrong—broken." Jessica, a nineteen-year-old woman, received an empathetic nod among the circle of college students I met with at Green Mountain College in Vermont. I was leading an empowerment workshop, "Where Passion Meets Success—Your Voice, Your Choice, Live on Purpose." My mission was and is to encourage young adults to create valuable, fulfilling lives by choosing a path based on what matters to them most. In many ways you could say I was preaching to the choir. I had immediate faith in this free-spirited, self-possessed bunch, and yet it was clear that they did not feel at ease with their world and questioned whether they could make a difference. Jessica was majoring in environmental studies. She was motivated by a spark of hope, yet daunted when she witnessed how institutions in her world seemed to operate and what many adults around her seemed to value. She felt discouraged about being able to have any effect after leaving Green Mountain.

Through my work as a spiritual activist, musician, and mentor I meet many Jessicas. They're often among the Millennial generation, but they share a feeling widely permeating the human spirit. Eight years ago, I actualized a dream I had to create a New

Year's Day Musical Odyssey to release the past, align with the present, and set the tone for the year ahead, using the power of the collective voice. Anyone who wanted to come was welcome. You did not have to be a trained singer. There were no rehearsals. It would not be scripted music. Rather, we would create spontaneous, wordless choruses in the moment from our intentions with the accompaniment of my acoustic instruments: crystal singing bowls, drums, and flute. I hung a few posters and advertised it on my website. I submitted a free listing to my local paper and crossed my fingers that a few people would show up. More than 100 people walked through the door that evening, packing the yoga studio. The invitation clearly struck and continues to strike a chord in people. The soundscape we generated was profoundly beautiful, the syntheses of our grief, gratitude, longing, and hope.

That gathering spawned my life's work which is to support spiritual seekers in restoring authority to their one true voice to create well-being in their lives and in the life of the world. For the past ten years, I have been offering live interactive musical events, virtual and in-person support groups and classes, restorative retreats and intensives, one-on-

one mentoring, as well as speaking and performing at conferences, community centers, and colleges under the brand name of One True Voice.

So many of the people I meet along the way express a longing to manifest a life that aligns with their unique interests and talents, but that also benefits the world. A surprising percentage of them admit that if they could, they would choose to do something altogether different with their time than what they do. Yet, they feel the world does not support them in following their dreams. Many college students think they should choose a major based on what will provide the maximum salary when they graduate, rather than based on their interests. Time and time again I hear people of all ages express their dissidence with the world, as well as a feeling of powerlessness to change its conditions.

Yet following our dreams and giving authority to the imaginal being within us to steward our lives may be just the action required to create personal success and the better world we imagine. We need your full participation. Are you with me so far? First, let's

examine the Dispirited Dream that seems to be holding us bound to a world that many of us say we would not willingly choose.

Descartes, "I think; therefore I am."

THOUGH WE'RE NOT PHYSICALLY THE STRONGEST species on the planet, we have become the most powerful, thanks to our ability to think—conceptualize, analyze, differentiate, and separate. This remarkable capacity to think has led to inventions and innovations that give us immediate access to unprecedented amounts of information and let us communicate at lightning speed across the globe to other people we may never meet in person. Our capacity to think has endowed us with many gifts, but when held without check it also can become a great liability and source of immense suffering.

Influential author of *The Power of Now* Eckhart Tolle suggests that though we are meant to possess thought, it's more accurate to say that thought possesses us. Unable to quiet the incessant mental noise, we become imprisoned by a compulsion to think. A simple aliveness that is actually natural to

us, an inborn quality of being in the moment which provides a fundamental ease and fulfillment, has been gravely compromised. Many of us feel as if we are no longer living in the fullness of who we are but instead have manifested a painful, hyper-materialistic world in which we are driven to seek fulfillment in things that can never satiate what we genuinely long for. The airbrushed self-image, the numerous gadgets, and the constant stimulation have not quelled our deeper hunger to live an inspired life, guided by our own authority, our unique passion and shared compassion. A vast dimension of our being that our calculating minds cannot quantify has been largely devalued or delegated to the realm of religion, which can devolve into a set of theological arguments that further alienate us from our true mission.

Shifts Happen

A MASS AWAKENING of human consciousness is simultaneously occurring. In fact, Our Dispirited Dream may be catalyzing the immense pressure and suffering that can spur enlightenment. Creating a nightmare, in other words, can force

us to awaken. Technologically amped up, relating far more to our iPhones than to one another, we stand on the threshold of personal and global crisis. But seeping through the cracks in the pavement, bleeding through our idling screen savers, and heard in the almost imperceptible silence between the roaring of engines, the human spirit is letting us know.

Humanity, as a whole, is on an evolutionary vision quest, its own rite of passage. And, as with any genuine rite of passage, the outcome is unknown, though many people purport that our survival as a species hangs in the balance. We have colluded with a world that denies our true nature, making it an unsustainable world. In our growing up as a species, it is time to realize that we, as individuals, have an ability and an accountability to affect a new reality. We need you.

We can look to the Achuar People and their prophecy of the Eagle and the Condor, for an illustration of the tension between the intellectual and intuitive capacities currently at odds within us. The Achuar People, also known as the 'Dream People' of the Amazon, are an indigenous group living in the Peruvian and Ecuadorian Rainforest. Having had no contact with the modern world until the 1970's, their isolation from Western society enabled them to preserve their intrinsic way of life. In their cosmology, dreams are highly valuable resources that affect and inform their waking lives. It is common practice to meet in small groups in the hours before sunset each morning to share and interpret their dreams. They believe that they dream not only for themselves but also for the community as a whole.

The Achuar have been highly influenced by an ancient Andean and Amazonian prophecy of The Eagle and The Condor.

The Eagle represents the intellect and cognitive capacities, and the Condor reflects the intuitive and compassionate side of our nature. This prophecy foretold of a time when there would be a great division within human consciousness. In the 500-year period between 1490 and 1990, it was said that the Eagle would dominate and threaten the very existence of the Condor. Our predilection to think would essentially conquer our capacity to dream the world into being. The prophecy went on to

explain that the era following, the time we find ourselves in now, would provide a golden opportunity for the Eagle and Condor to fly again in the same sky. The Achuar believe that humanity's future survival, though not guaranteed, depends on the two to coexist in mutual respect and balance with one another.

Note this example of how the Condor and Eagle can fly together in real time: When the modern world's demand for oil and pollution from drilling began encroaching upon the Achuar's land and waterways, the Achuar reached out in hopes of halting the destruction. The Pachamama Alliance was formed with a group of concerned Westerners, and the two worlds embarked on a mission to not only stop further desecration of the rainforest, but also to shift human consciousness in a new direction. In their interaction with the outside world, the Achuar shamans and elders observed a dream underlying our behavior, and they urged us that without changing this fundamental dream, no actions taken on the surface would have an enduring effect. The Pachamama Alliance has become a highly influential global community, dedicated to changing the dream of humanity. They have aimed to do so by merging indigenous wisdom with modern-world knowledge to achieve their mission of bringing forth "an environmentally sustainable, spiritually fulfilling, socially just human presence on this planet." Their efforts have been integral in preserving indigenous lands and culture. They also have brought to the surface some of the most pressing issues confronting us today.

Ceding the Old Stories

Cultural myths subtly shape how we view ourselves and our purpose in this lifetime. They influence how we relate to each other and what we value. To shift from our current Dispirited Dream we must shift our perception of ourselves at the very root, and redefine who we are in relationship to our universe. Before we can do this, we have to become fully aware of the current defining myths that color our perceptions, affect our behavior, and influence our decision-making.

The Story of "I'm separate."

Our modern world cosmology emphasizes the myth of separation. We are conditioned to separate from our own nature, from one another, and from the natural world around us. We meticulously classify ourselves into four races with 30 subgroups, then further by nationality, political, and religious belief, gender, and so on, when in fact we share 99.99+% of the same genetic material with all other human beings. Beneath this preoccupation with our differences is a hidden fear-driven doctrine that your success and well-being detract from mine. Maybe the opposite is true.

Renowned 20th-century inventor and visionary R. Buckminster Fuller says that to create a sustainable planet we must go from a "you *or* me" world to a

"you *and* me" world. In a "you or me" world we have to expend a great deal of our life force competing with one another to insure our personal security, the precept that renders us capable of killing and enslaving our own species. We are taught to measure our worth against other people and societal standards. We value prestige over personal growth.

This cultural myth reflects a separation we feel deeply within. While we are wired to follow our distinct interests and instincts, many of us learn to devalue that impulse, separating from our inner guidance, the one true voice within us. We are taught to give authority to what we think and distrust what we feel. The visionary is banished to the unconscious even though she is vital in guiding us to our most valuable contribution. We live according to someone else's clock and play outwardly dictated roles, forcing ourselves into jobs and lifestyles that do not reflect our unique preferences. We neglect our creativity and squander our gifts. This disconnect from our true nature keeps us from seeing our greater purpose and the rippling consequences of our actions that affect other people, other creatures, and the planet at large—our greater family.

The Story of 'I don't have enough.'

Like you, somewhere along the way, I received the shocking message that I was inadequate, flawed, not good enough. I cannot say precisely how, when, or by whom the message was delivered but perfectionism was my coping strategy. I measured myself against impossible standards and unconsciously believed that if I could just attain perfection, my security would be insured.

The story of "not enough" is deeply woven into our collective psyche, professed in every advertisement goading us to buy some cosmetic product, medicine, or retirement plan. Even those who possess fame and fortune, or who meet the cultural ideal standards of physical beauty, struggle with this. In a "not-enough" culture, survival becomes the primary objective and another cause for turning away from what matters most deeply to us. This dogma of lack fuels our greed, causing us to take too much, hoard, binge, overuse, deplete resources, and manipulate others. We have to be vigilant that others do not take our share. We end up

worshipping stuff and bowing to our economy as an authority to monitor and ration resources, which in turn affects our personal happiness and well-being. I have fallen for this myth many times, having numerous days when the number in my bank account could set me into a pit of despair even though other things in my life were going very well.

Fear and greed are not natural. They're learned, at least according to author of *Of Human Wealth* Bernard Lietaer, contemporary European author, former senior officer of Belgian Central Bank, and one of the chief officers of the Euro currency. The Achuar called the dream that possessed us "a dream of more." Our dispirited myths can easily obscure the true root of our problems. The World Hunger Project research shows that the world currently grows enough food to feed the world over. Our hunger problem, though

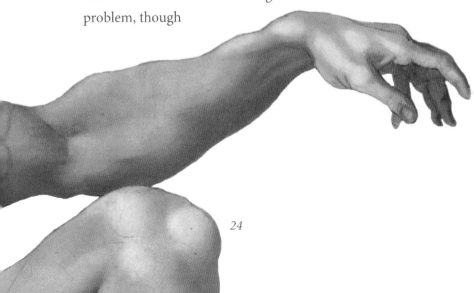

commonly perceived as a scarcity of resources, is actually caused by human greed.

The Story of "I can't."

My first introduction to God was as this old white guy who lived in the sky, who seemed not to like me much. He was portrayed as angry and yet it was impressed upon me that I should love him. As a child, I found this portrait confusing. It was unnatural for me to love this kind of god.

Whether you were educated religiously or not, Western civilization is influenced by Judeo-Christian religious myths, many of which relegate much authority to an outer God. Remnants of delegating authority to an external authority are still alive within our collective psyche. We assume the role of child in a universe controlled by an outer, harsh, punishing force. We struggle to own our own power and are a bit confused about who is really in charge of our lives. We have inherited the illusory dream of our predecessors who believed in an outer force to make decisions and determine our destiny. This entrenched perspective leads us to believe that we are powerless to change the conditions of our world. And this story contributes to our unaccountability for our actions, as if someone else, some unknown parental force in charge, will come and clean up the mess.

I tell you, no one is coming. We will be the ones to change the dream.

The Story of 'We have to go along to get along'

In the fifth grade I loved writing in cursive and secretly considered myself a master. One day on a math quiz in a self-possessed, lighthearted gesture, I wrote my name on the designated line at the top of my test.

Never imagining anyone would care, I crafted a celebratory "Y" at the end of my name, the stem of which extended well beyond the prescribed loops and curves. A few mornings later, to my shock, I was the target of public shaming by the fifth-grade nun, for what I could only assume was the sin of my self-expression.

Our Dispirited Dream demands conformity. I think of all the voices along the way that advised me to conform. There was my high school guidance counselor cautioning me against the dangers of art school because she was convinced it would lead to life-long poverty. I recall pressure from in-laws to get a 'real' job. I remember the painful decree from my financial counselor post-divorce that I should expect to struggle, that my only chance for salvation would be to pressure my co-parent for the maximum alimony and child support charges.

All these voices condemned the inspired path, fearfully urging me to choose a well-traveled one—butcher, baker, candle stick maker—not musician, mentor, spiritual activist, and gong player. Despite my great fortune of being born to parents who encouraged me to do what I wanted with my life, I struggled against the cultural messages of conformity. I suffered with chronic depression from childhood into my early adulthood. I remember my father trying to tell me as kindly as he could that I had inherited the unfortunate gene for depression epidemic in my family, that it was "chemical" and something I would unfortunately have to struggle with the rest of my life. I heard stories about aunts and uncles, shades drawn, whose lives were destroyed by it. I felt as though I had received a death sentence.

The visionary inside me could not accept such a decree upon my life, and the conditioned self dreaded it was true.

I am now convinced that depression is for many of us a spiritual response to having to diminish the dreamer, the imaginal self within to whom conforming literally means death—the death of one's purpose and one's mission.

Stephen Cope shares this quote from Krishna in the Bhagavad Gita: "The attempt to live out someone else's dharma brings extreme spiritual peril." Once I was truly able to live according to my own dream, my own dharma, once I allowed

a new story to define my life, then the chronic, allegedly inevitable, chemical, familial depression disappeared altogether and has not returned.

I wonder how these myths have played out in your life and limited your ability to actualize your most inspired dreams? We are heirs to a Dispirited Dream. It promises an illusory security if we conform. It is time we see that going along does not serve us. There is a much deeper security available to us.

Though, evolutionarily speaking, non-peace is the new normal, I do not believe it is our natural state. As we empower a new identity and a new story, I believe we will again become highly sensitive to any state of non-peace. Try asking yourself these two questions next time you find yourself there:

What do I fear most?

What am I telling myself that I cannot have that deeply matters to me?

You might find that ultimately the fear links back to you not being able to be you in this world. To successfully shift from a world that does not reflect our true nature to a world we would deliberately choose, it is essential to excavate these negative story lines ingested from our current cosmology. Let's review some of the major ones:

We fear we live in a dangerous and punitive world.

We fear we have to expend a great deal of energy to stay safe.

We fear our making our way in the world is a battle and that we best seek the security of the known path.

We fear we do not have authority to choose what we do with our lives.

We fear that what matters to us most won't matter to others.

And perhaps that is just an illusion. And perhaps we can dream another world.

part three

*An Imaginal
Reality*

ALTHOUGH I CAN IMAGINE and viscerally feel a new dream for humanity, I was having difficulty putting words to it. I went to bed asking for a dream. That night, I dreamt that I was looking into the face of another woman. We were silent, but after a few moments she opened her mouth and out flew a butterfly. Next, I opened my mouth, and a butterfly flew out. No words. Just a delicate winged being whose imaginal body, soft as rose petals, left a wonderful feeling in my mouth. The dream was a profound experience in and of itself, and it provided just the images for the words I needed.

In the chrysalis, the caterpillar turns to liquid and produces new cells that zoologists refer to as their "imaginal" cells. These cells give the caterpillar its power to transform into a butterfly, an imaginal insect, which is an insect in its adult stage after metamorphosis. Archetypal Psychology uses the term metaphorically to describe a fully realized human being.

An "Imaginal Reality" mirrors our vibrational essence; the balance of the mystical and metaphysical dimension of our being with the tangible and material dimension. Even the word "human" reflects this dual nature in its two syllable, HU and MAN. HU comes to us from the Persian language, and refers to 'spirit'—that divine, ineffable, immaterial essence; that great mystery that lives within us and that we live within. MAN comes from Sanskrit for 'mind' and refers to the ordinary—our visible, physical, material nature. Spirit and mind merged create the human being. In a world biased toward the material and the tangible, it is vital for us to reclaim this union as our full identity.

We are imaginal beings. We have come to transform. We intended to leave this world better than the way we found it and we are here to dream BIG. We need you to heed your dreams. You are dreaming for all of us, you know.

When I graduated from college, I had dreams of going to the West Coast to earn my Master's degree. I filled out applications and acquired letters of recommendation, but I backed out due to the simple fact that I was terribly afraid of the unknown. I chose instead to accept an invitation to live with my boyfriend in New York City. We married a year later. He was and still is a supportive and generous man, and a good friend to me. We had three children together, whom I cherish in this world above all else.

By my late 20's, I was a parent, a partner, a householder, and a small business owner. We had a nice home, enough money. I was living the dream by cultural standards, and yet, anxiety and depression stalked me, compounded by the feeling that they were totally unjustified, as on the surface I had everything. I was haunted by a restlessness that there was another life for me, something else I needed or wanted to be doing. But threatened by these feelings, I admitted them to no one—not my sister, my best friend, my therapist, let alone myself. I feared hurting and disappointing those I loved most. I feared losing my security.

I began having recurring dreams that my shoes were too small. I'd sift through piles by the door, searching for a pair that fit. Sometimes I would settle for a pair that was too small or did not match. Often, I would surrender and go barefoot, but when I would open the door to leave the house I would discover that all the buildings had collapsed. I would stand there frozen, unable to move beyond the doorway, even though the

landscape beyond the door had a peaceful stillness and was brightly lit by the sun. In my dream life, I was trying to resolve what I could not face in my waking reality—that I had created a life for myself that was seemingly perfect, but as it turned out, not perfect for me. This was far too sad of a recognition for me at the time, with what I thought would be earth-shattering consequences.

As consciousness awakens, and we step toward a more realized self, previously held images that are too small or have deviated too far from our essential truth begin to collapse. This can occur on a personal and grand scale. At such transitional times in our personal lives, we may find ourselves in chaos—disoriented, restless, ill, or no longer fitting into our current profession, lifestyle, or relationships the way we once did. On a mass scale, we see widespread evidence of such symptoms—a pervasive restlessness, increased violence, and the dramatic disruption and breakdown of established systems.

Many of us are becoming acutely aware of the pain that results from living misaligned with ourselves. You will be offering a great gift to the whole by instead discovering through what you love the gift you have to bring. We need you. But, how do you do it? Well, first it requires that you get intimately acquainted with the part of you that guides your own distinct mission in this life.

Now is the time.

Calling on the Imaginal Self

"What you fear is an indication of what you seek"

—Thomas Merton

As far back in my childhood as I can remember, I had day dreams of myself singing on stage. Encased in white light within a smoky darkness, I could completely imagine myself passionately engaged with an audience and deeply in the zone, musically. In my waking reality, however, I was painfully shy and self-conscious, by no stretch an obvious performer. More apt to torture an audience than inspire them, I was fearful of being seen or heard, which caused involuntary, noticeable dry mouth and a wild quivering of my voice. I learned early on to avoid anything vaguely resembling the limelight. Though I melted countless hours at

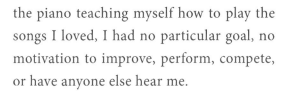

the piano teaching myself how to play the songs I loved, I had no particular goal, no motivation to improve, perform, compete, or have anyone else hear me.

But music captivated me and put me into a state of wonder and timelessness. I was magnetically drawn to those keys but too anxious to study with a teacher. I was a closet singer, saving my pennies to buy sheet music, a walking athenaeum of song lyrics, but never one of those kids tap dancing for her aunts and uncles or singing in school plays.

Yet, there was a visionary inside me, a watching and witnessing presence wholeheartedly drawn to that light, born to commune and express herself with ease and comfort. This imaginal self accompanied me from the start and has resided in me since, though she was exiled for a time to the back room of my awareness. Any surfacing of such dreams in my adolescence or early adulthood I dismissed as that of a generic wannabe-rockstar fantasy.

43

In my early 30s, I began studying yoga. The school I joined offered special events, one of which was a chanting night in which we sang mantras from a yoga tradition. At the time I found it odd but compelling. Within weeks, I purchased a hand drum, surprised to discover I had a natural affinity for playing. I continued to be involved in these events, and though I avoided it for as long as I could, there came a time when I was asked to sing a small, solo part. Me? Sing? Solo? I hesitantly accepted, which must have stirred my imaginal cells. Like a genie bursting from a tarnished imprisonment, the dreamer materialized in full, colorful reality before me, petitioning my wish.

A torrent of great love and simultaneous terror unleashed in me. Stifled notes and choked phrases puffed from my vocal chords. I felt crushed. The voice that emerged was not my genuine voice.

That moment triggered a profound longing in me to liberate my voice and release the cage from around my heart that seemed to hold it captive. It was a tremendous threat to the conditioned self, who dismissed such a mission as absurd. And the threat was justified as emancipating the dreamer after a life-long suppression was the initial impetus that set nearly

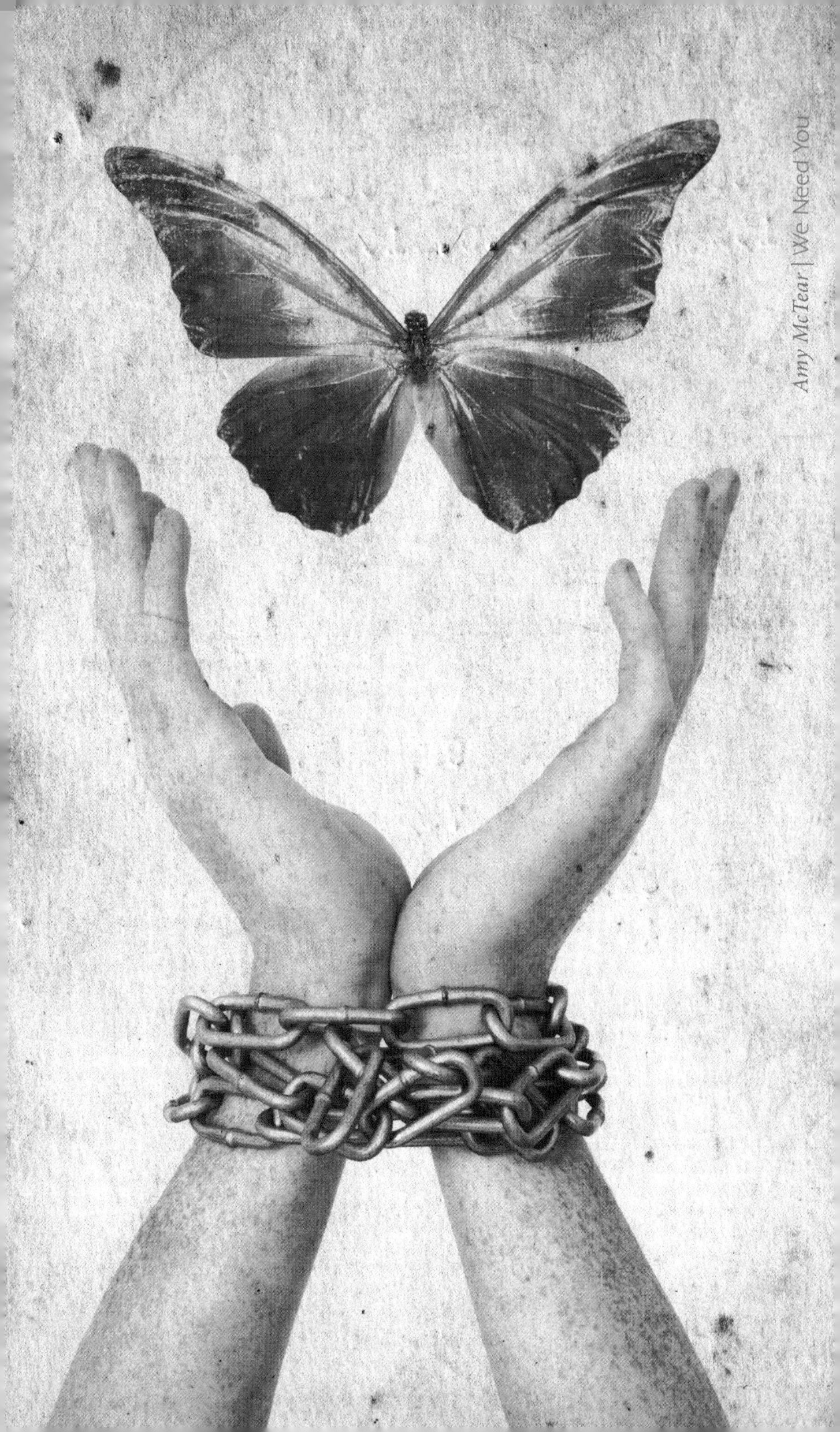

Amy McTear | We Need You

every aspect of my tangental life toppling to the ground. At this intense crossroad, I could try to squash the dreamer back into her tiny lamp or integrate her into my life and, dammit, I liked her.

Rumi says, *"There is some kiss we want with our whole lives—the touch of spirit on the body."* Spirit pierced my safe prison and kissed me in one available, fleeting moment. Singing ignited something in me, and though I felt terribly estranged from my voice, I longed to kiss life in this way.

Everyone has a visionary, the keeper of a sacred vision, a greater intelligence alerting us along the way to a bigger picture and purpose. If unrestricted, we manifest in our own befitting manner, sometimes in absolutely unreasonable ways, or I should say, for reasons beyond our capacity to comprehend rationally.

Sadly, Our Dispirited Dream often conditions us to conform to a safe path rather than journey through the unknown in resonance with the one true voice within us. We are guided to choose one of the sanctioned roles, instead of unfolding our own. This outwardly authorized path, this siren song of security, holds hostage our highest potential, our most valuable contribution, and ultimately, our wellbeing.

My recurring dream of crowded shoes and demolished buildings began manifesting in my waking reality. I could no longer maintain my grip on a life that was not truly mine. I was eventually pushed across the threshold into the ruin of everything I clung to—my marriage, my family life, my career and my future plans. Those were some of the most challenging and painful years of my life, but in hindsight some of the most important. I mourned illusions of safety and surrendered my allegiance to a life half-lived. I found myself scouring the wreckage for my own remains, searching for some indestructible shred of me that might have given me a clue to who I really was.

As messy and painful as it was, I was blessed with a second chance to reimagine my life and realign with the deeper, more authentic dream of who I was. In that time of dissolution, I observed I was not alone. I saw all of us as a multitude of spiritual refugees fleeing the oppression of our own distorted nightmare, our Dispirited Dream, in which the Eagle has flown solo too long to its own detriment. Some of us are just trying to get along; some of us, giving up; some of us, fighting hard to reclaim an existence that reflects and nurtures our most authentic nature.

Within The Great Net

We can envision a new world by looking at an ancient story. Our Hindu ancestors have a creation story thousands of years old, telling of the great thunderbolt god, Indra, who is said to live at the center of the universe. In the beginning of time, Indra crafted a net, placing a shining gem at each juncture, the facets of which reflected in every other. Casting this net in every direction over creation, each gem became a human soul, simultaneously

unique while also infinitely reflecting every other jewel in the web. Any change in one produced a change, however small, in all of the others.

This ancient myth explained the workings of our universe, illustrating the symphony of cause and effect that governs our world. According to this cosmology, all living beings are inextricably linked within a great network, not only to one another but also to the matrix itself. Each is simultaneously held by the web while also accountable to it. What each does, however brightly or dimly each reflects, directly effects the overall brightness of the web. Implied within this creation myth is the notion that if every one brings forth with clarity and fullness what they have within, whether subtle or highly visible, that all the needs of the web are covered. Psychologist Stephen Cope notes in his book *The Great Work of Your Life*, "This is why we all have different dharmas [life purposes]. Every base is covered somehow, but only if everyone acts on their authentic calling. Only if everyone holds together her part of the net."

How would it be if we had been taught from early on that we are a single but vital note in a vast, cosmic symphony? What if this were the fundamental theme that ran throughout our nursery rhymes and childhood stories? Imagine your parents and your teachers powering home the message that your most sacred task in this life is to discover what matters to you most and create value from it—and consider that contribution not as yours alone but as a singular contribution to the interconnected net of life. How would this change how you live each day?

"The World is as you Dream it."—John Perkins

Halfway through my fourth decade on the planet, I can attest that my dreams have come true—some I wanted and some I did not want. I realize now that if I dreamt it enough, it became my reality. What we look for, we see. Each of us is positioned at different coordinates on the net, and, therefore, we each view the world through a slightly different lens. At the same time, there is much of reality that we agree upon, being that we share the net. In both cases, the world is a reflection of our image of the world. If we are focused on what we fear, what we hate, how we are inadequate, then our outer reality reflects that, and we will discover a world filled with that. If our awareness is centered on what inspires us, those are the images that materialize around us. This is one way we create worlds with our thoughts, feelings, and actions. Our inborn capacity to effect the larger web endows us with an important and vital role in the creation of our universe. So, be mindful of what you dream. You just might make it so in your reality.

"How do we change the world?
Change the story."—Charles Eisenstein

Working Out Illusions

Recently, I started working out at a gym. All workout equipment faces four television screens. Each screen perpetuates images from our Dispirited Dream. There is the channel that streams one violent drama after the next, fueling the fear that we live in a dangerous and punitive world. Another that promotes an exhaustive array of beauty products, fashions and diets, promising to make us adequate. And a third that reinforces the story of separation with 24/7 news of war, social conflict, and political debate. Safe to assume, we all were at the gym with a common desire for improved health, yet inadvertently we were filling up on the broken world stories. After several months of working out in front of these screens, I felt remarkably up to speed on world events and pop culture, but that saturation challenged my ability to focus positively on my life and the world I choose to dream into being. I decided, instead, to keep my eyes off the screen. I also experimented with streaming audible recordings of positive affirmations into my headphones. Listening to positive affirmations was new for me, but I found them to be an effective tool for replacing defeating narratives.

Timothy Wilson, professor of psychology at the University of Virginia and author of the book *Redirect*, refers to the process of improving our lives by changing our personal stories about ourselves and our world, as "story editing." One of his well-researched methods for doing so he calls 'Do good, be good', the premise of which is that we can change our story by first changing our behavior. Wilson says this approach goes back to the time of Aristotle, who said, "We become just by the practice of just actions, self-controlling by exercising self-control, and courageous by performing acts of courage." Spiritual teacher and channel Abraham-Hicks offers a similar "fake it until you make it" approach, asserting that 'acting as if it is already so' is often the necessary first step in improving the conditions of our lives. Abraham-Hicks points out that the underlying belief, rather than words themselves, are the true factor in attracting our life circumstances. However, Abraham also clarifies that the statements, whether in conversation or as thoughts in our heads, have much to do with reinforcing our beliefs and determining our state of being. This could explain why certain research has indicated that positive affirmations can have a paradoxical effect and actually increase negativity in people who have acute low self-esteem or have suffered extreme trauma. People in this category were said to have improvements more readily when they were allowed their negative thoughts. Changing our story requires a combination of the cognitive work as well as a focus on choosing new thoughts and behaviors. We disempower underlying negative narratives by making them fully conscious, understanding how they operate in our lives, and seeing them from a distance, so that we can break our identification with them. We then empower a new reality by empowering a new belief. Positive affirmations can be a helpful part of this.

Lori was my client who first came to see me when she was in her late 60s. She had a delicate physique and a swallowed quality to her voice. She was burdened by a heavy past and a deep frustration that she did not have the courage to assert herself in her life. We spent a great deal of time exploring her history, identifying the repeated themes and the defeating internal voices that seemed to color her present interactions. After many months, it became clear that continuing to discuss these negative events in her life only seemed to strengthen them. I suggested we turn our conversations toward her positive qualities, what she liked about herself, as well as the positive aspects of her life. I invited her to share her wildest dreams with me—what she dreamed of doing with her life, who she dreamed of being. It was amazing to witness her voice strengthen and change in quality during these discussions. In describing her dreams for her life, we created one stipulation—that she speak in the present tense, as if it were already so. Lori began observing a significant improvement in how she felt. She implemented Abraham-Hicks's practices like writing note pages of her good attributes and what she loved about her life. Gradually she began expanding her horizons. Where she was once frightened to drive her car locally, she was now taking trips to the Amazon. In her travels, she met a man and fell in love. She ended up moving across the country and marrying him. And now into her 70s, no exaggeration, all I see is one Facebook post after the next of her hang gliding and riding motorcycles. Truly, she is one of my all-time heroes.

Lori is a great student of life. She learned something vital for us all to learn—that she alone has domain over her response to her world. She learned that what she looked for, she would see and so she took the reins and decided to look for the life that she wanted to be living, in the world she wanted to be living it in. The paradise we seek is a parallel reality to our Dispirited Dream, waiting for us to see it and choose it. We need to realize that we are perpetuating the conditions of our world with our focus and that we can shift our focus to the preferred conditions.

"One of the ways that your project, your personal healing, or your social invention can change the world is through story. But even if no one ever learns of it, even if it is invisible to every human on Earth, it will have no less of an effect."
—Charles Eisenstein

What are your big dreams? I invite you to call them from the back room of your awareness, where you too may have secreted them away some time ago. Reflect on them, write about them, clarify the vision, take ownership, share them with someone also capable of holding a big vision.

Dream away, and as you do observe the internalized voices that question your authority to do so. Don't let these voices take you over and convince you that they are you. They are the voices of your conditioning. At the same time, do not resist them. Get to know them thoroughly and intimately. Here's why:

Your One True Voice

We are all equipped with a 24/7 internal guidance system, tirelessly doing its best to signal us as we interact with our world through our tastes, attractions, imagination, and personal interests. But we internalize a lot of dramatic voice-over that obscures its guidance. A cast of characters takes up residency within us, where there was originally just one.

With my clients and myself, I have found it is helpful to step back and begin to personify the crew inside. As you might guess, this process can bring its share of comic relief. You likely will find a lively bunch in there, some grandiose voices, some diminishing and cruel voices, some helpless and submissive voices— but all too often, voices that are in discord with one another. Yet, by personifying them, you will soon be able to predict with precision who will show up when and exactly what they will say. Have a good time portraying them as vividly as you can. One of my leading cast members is a starving orphan with holes in her shoes unwilling to relinquish her victim mentality. A client of mine personified one of his most persistent internal trouble-makers as a fierce gargoyle with a nose ring guarding the gate of his heart. Look for these sub-personalities in the troubled arenas of your life and notice the reels and story lines that they tell. *Inside Out,* a 3-D computer-animated a film released in 2015 illustrated this internal drama beautifully. The film is set in the mind of a young girl, Riley Andersen, in which five personified emotions—Joy, Sadness, Fear, Anger, and Disgust—try to guide her through life during a traumatic move to a new city. While each is vying for central command in Riley's "headquarters", Riley in the end learns how to maintain ultimate control while accepting and befriending the presence of each of them.

Once aware of the crew you keep, you can begin to break your unconscious identification with them. You are less persuaded by their urgency and are free to act and speak without their burdensome influence. The crew inside is no longer running the show, and you are far more capable of identifying and being guided by your one true voice.

As you observe the cacophony of inner voices, ask yourself, "Who is this one voice that is observing the others?" This is your one true voice. The one true voice is the pure consciousness that contains all the other voices. When we witness with neutrality, we are engaging our pure awareness or consciousness, the aggregate that holds all the others. We encounter the authentic self and can begin to identify with the inner guidance that leads us to our purpose and our genuine fulfillment. We expand our creative freedom and our capacity to live out of character. We reclaim the power to change the story and dissolve patterns that keep us from our true path.

Seeding New Stories

I have performed several Summer Solstice concerts in a local former cement mine called the Widow Jane Mine, an awe-inspiring cavernous room, with huge monolithic stone pillars and booming acoustics. At the height of summer, we descend into the heart of the earth and engage musically, mindfully, and meditatively to empower our personal and collective intentions. Our intention is to emerge renewed, reconnected, more clear about our personal direction and inspired to do our part in bettering our world. These events have grown to include audiences in the hundreds, as well as up to twenty-five performers, including a group of drummers, a choir, and several musicians.

In 2012, I thought it would be a great idea to open the event by singing a dramatic solo invocation, an original composition I created blending English and Arabic lyrics with a creative, get this—scream with wild abandon at the end. Singing solo in front of an audience that large was new for me at that time. When I got to the venue that day, I wondered *"what the hell I had been thinking."* As people were entering the cave, a scourge of internal banter was forecasting a terrible outcome. Looking towards the ticket entrance, I saw a man enter who had kindly accepted my personal invitation. He was a highly successful world-class vocalist who tours the world. I was romantically interested in him, which, admittedly, was largely why I invited him, and now this guy would hear me scream. Next, a group of my clients that I was working with in a group came in together, aglow with excitement. The crew inside me was in a full frenzy. I was convinced I'd lose everyone's respect after this. I felt incredibly vulnerable but came to when I remembered these voices were not the whole of me. I knew if I let the cacophony of fearful characters lead the show, I would be disheartened at the outcome. I also knew there was no way to evict them.

So here is what I did: I imagined I could hold my vulnerability in my left hand and my power in my right as equal partners. As, the cave fell silent and it was time to begin, I took the long walk to the microphone, aware of both hands. Staring into the darkness I could no longer make out the faces, but I knew that cave was holding hundreds of vulnerable hearts. I told myself I would sing to every one of them, as if this might be my last chance ever to kiss life in this way. My voice quivered but with authenticity, and a powerful fragility.

Here is one of the many messages I received the next day:

"That was quite a spectacular event you arranged and what a venue! It was my first experience of

the caves, and an unforgettable one. Your spoken words captured the essence of this time of alarming, startling, awakening transition beautifully and your singing voice was the strongest and most free I have ever heard it!"

I overcame stage fright by adjusting the lens through which I viewed those viewing me. Instead of feeding my fears that I was innately flawed and had to prove my worth, I saw everyone in the audience as another me. I saw myself as them, too—both vulnerable and powerful, dubious and hopeful, at the heart of it all, each doing our best to navigate the challenges of courageously claiming our full nature. Embodying this storyline, I was able to drop pretense and not waste my life force striving for other people to validate my worth. I identified instead with the soul of why I get on stage—to connect meaningfully and send whatever positive wave I can into the greater net. I do this for my own well-being.

As a world, we are hungry for a new paradigm. We are at a breaking point with living out of integrity with ourselves. We long to live meaningful lives and align with our purpose and a purpose beyond ourselves. Are you ready for a new story to guide your life and define your world?

You belong

If you could fly above with the Eagle and the Condor, you would witness your unquestionable membership in the cosmic verse. You are constantly effected and effecting, undeniably woven into an ecosystem, a food chain, eating and being eaten, hosting and being hosted by many other life forms at all times. Your living, in whatever minuscule way, impacts the ecology — the soil, the flow of rivers, the cleanliness of oceans, and the quality of air. Flying above, you would see how your ideas and emotions rapidly reverberate along a human circuit. You would witness how many acts of cruelty are stopped with your one small, conscious refusal to pass on the suffering. You would have compassion for how difficult it is for us to resist the wave of collective fear and pain. Our experience of separation would be recognized for what it is, at the least greatly exaggerated and arguably illusory.

You have everything you need

We live on an abundant planet, easily a paradise, in which the cure continuously grows alongside the disease and in which problems coexist with solutions. We have the capacity to empower a marvelous coexistence with our natural resources. We have easily enough intelligence to solve distribution problems, grow food in many different climates, clean up the damage to our water, and restore our people and planet to health. We also have everything within us to unfold our personal mission and deliver our most valuable

contribution. When the underlying dream changes, when we successfully remove the blinders of the old cosmological conditioning, we will be able to apply our collective intelligence to its most enlightened purpose. Our lives will speak to us again with clarity and without the manipulation of fear attempting to protect itself from the distorted dream.

You can

Within every human being resides an artist. Our lives are the clay. You are a creator by your most fundamental nature. You were born into this world in a state of wonder, wired to immediately reach out, interact, and impact. The world is missing something that you want to bring, and you were born equipped to give it. If you love it, you will in some way discover some hidden talent or gift related to it.

When you live your dharma, when you walk your walk with integrity, people sense it and are drawn to you. When you do what you care about most, you bring far more value than when you attach yourself to something of lesser importance

to you. Setting out on a course for your unique life, there is an incomplete picture before you, awaiting your input. You have authority. You are meant to take risks, try different things, put out invitations, mess up, fall down, tolerate feeling lost, doubt your sanity. Experiencing this enables you to make choices, to see what your preferences are and what does and does not suit you. To be a rock star, you do not need to be born one. To go for something, it is not a requirement that you excelled at it in school.

Can you see the incredible palette before you, a precious canvas within which to create? Your collaborators near and far are seeking you as you seek them. This is the inherent joy of being, your fulfillment and the magic of co-creating a world.

You Choose

Though I was conditioned to believe that to be a valuable person I had to choose based on what was socially acceptable, I now understand that we are meant to choose our path based on what matters to us most.

"This turning toward what you deeply love saves you," 13th century Sufi poet Rumi notes, "Read the book of your life which has been given you. A voice comes to your soul saying — lift your foot, cross over, move into emptiness of question and answer and question. The quest never ends."

Followers of Rumi, the Mevlevis or "Whirling Dervish," practice a form of spinning to turn their consciousness toward light and love, relinquishing attachment to the ego's suffering and the hurtful impressions of the world. To avoid dizziness, they must find the center of the center in which they can contemplate their true being, as born out of the purity of their own heart.

When it comes time for us to make important life choices, we can practice *Turning*. When I say *Turning*, I mean the act of turning attention, as Rumi describes, toward what we most deeply love. When you choose based on what you love, from your own authority, you are far more likely to yield something of value. When you choose by trying to please others or attain security, you are more likely to experience drain, resentment, and confusion. You spread suffering.

"A thousand half loves must be forsaken in order to take one whole heart home," Rumi also says. The

"half loves," our fearful attachments to that which the fearless, fully actualized being in us would not choose, must be left behind in order to make our most generous contribution to this life, deliverance of the one true whole-hearted self.

Many people hover close to their true calling but stop short of fully living out their dharma in order to stay within the parameters of the norm. I once tried to get

other people to write the songs I didn't think I was capable of writing. I chose professions in the visual and healing arts but was afraid to step up to what excited me and scared me most. Remember Thomas Merton's quote, "What you fear is an indication of what you seek." Coming face-to-face with our dharma inspires a certain amount of fear in us. Our job is to cross the threshold to the deeper joy and security, as well as unexpected delights that await us. I encourage you to aim for the bullseye of your life calling, to keep moving to the center of the center, even when the voices get shrill and desperate. We need you to. Discovering your calling is a journey, but if we faithfully direct our feet in the direction of what inspires us, the light that we carry within that we pledged to share will be revealed. Allow yourself to be led there.

In the process of reclaiming my life, I reflected on what I love. It is a simple exercise. I highly recommend that you try it. Here is what I wrote years ago. It still holds true: "I love to explore the unseen, the mystery, the spiritual dimension of my being. I love to reflect on the journey of the human soul and unfold it like a mystery novel. I love to teach and inspire. I love to be immersed in natural beauty. I love deep emotional bonds. I love to explore unity with others musically and experience the power and vulnerability of my own voice." During those difficult years, when I found myself afraid I did not have enough, afraid I would have to do work in the world I did not love, afraid I would be without love… I practiced Turning. I conjured up and reconnected to the images of love and beauty that inspire me, the most profound vision for my life, that I had secreted away in the most tender chambers of my heart. I enabled the imaginal self, and I found life quickly responded. What I engaged with inside began to appear in many forms around me. By attuning to what we deeply love, we draw resonance from our outer environment. Not a rejection or denial of current reality, rather the nobel role of the Master, turning and tuning her life.

Turning toward what you truly love may require you to let go of much of the advice you've been given, and I know that includes mine. Whether you are a few years outside of high school or at a great turning point in your life's journey, this may be the nexus when it is essential for you to access inner authority and listen for your own voice. At its calling, you can follow your interests and decide what matters to you most. This will allow you to develop into the most potent version of you.

You are an integral part of this precious opportunity to take part in the collaboration of a world. Despite the cacophonous cast of characters inside and out, your one true voice continuously rallies you towards self-actualization. The universe or 'one song' awaits your note in the collective chorus.

part four
We Need You

YOU CARRY THE SEED of something wondrous. You came for your own evolution and to help us all evolve. Each of us lends a note to this greater symphony. In the last seven years of exploration into the writing and recording of music, I have observed many powerful parallels. Here are six musical metaphors designed to help you dream the world you want into being.

6 Ways to Actualize your Imaginal Reality

1. Find Your Key

Every piece of music has its own "key." The key is based on the central or most important pitch in the piece. All the other pitches are patterned off of this tone. This tone is often the note that begins and ends the song. James D'Angelo, in his book *The Healing Power of the Human Voice* shares a technique for finding what he calls "Your Fundamental Tone." I would describe this tone as the central or most comfortable note in your vocal range. D'Angelo believes that intentionally vocalizing this tone "sends sympathetic vibrations to the root, awakening the fine energy that assists in our spiritual unfolding." When I did this exercise years ago, I discovered my fundamental tone was Bb. I had a whole set of crystal singing bowls at this point, every half and whole note in the scale. Interestingly, Bb was the only bowl that I continuously ignored and left on the shelf. Go figure! I made a conscious effort after that to work with that bowl, and now I use it all the time as of course it is the easiest one for me to sing with.

So, what is the key for you? Where do your fundamental interests lie? What draws you? What captivates you? What do you care about most? Is it in the realm of music? Quantum theory? Carpentry? Marine biology? Latin Dance? What arena of life do you generally gravitate toward? Are you visual, cerebral, auditorily inclined? Just as the central pitch of the song is often the note the song begins and ends with, sometimes the first thing you ever wanted to be "when you grew up" holds a clue. And, conversely it also may be the thing you are currently avoiding or fearing, like that Bb bowl.

Make it a point to notice what puts you in that timeless state of wonder. What you are doing when you feel naturally energized? Also notice who you admire. Your one true voice alerts you when there is resonance near, even if it shows up in someone else. This also can manifest as envy. Pay attention to these envious feelings. They are great sign posts alerting you to something you are not claiming in yourself.

2. Feel for a Rhythm

In song recording, once you establish the key, then you lay down the support of a rhythm section and a bass line. This holds the structure for your song. Similarly, your basic life rhythm, how you live, spend your time and energy needs to match what you care about. Look for the cadence in life that suits you, and adjust as you get to know yourself better. Explore, engage, experiment in the realm of your interests, even during the period when you do not fully and clearly understand what it is. Just begin apprenticing with it in all the ways that you can. The human journey is a treasure hunt. Your life purpose rarely reveals itself overnight with perfect clarity. It is important to be curious and engage, to do something and start somewhere, let one step lead to another. This might mean accepting odd jobs related to your interests or doing volunteer work. Find the people who share your interests. Go

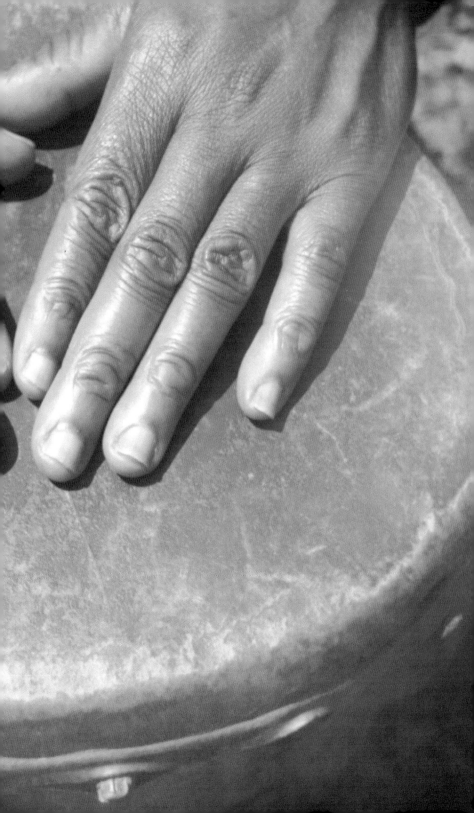

to places that excite you. Interview others whom you admire that do what you think you might love to be doing.

When I was in my 20's living in NYC, I was interested in anthropology and human origins, as I think I was searching for clues to understanding the human journey. I visited the Museum of Natural History by myself weekly. During that time, I bought a book, *The First Humans: Human Origins and History to 10,000 B.C.* by David Hurst Thomas. It was a large-format, fully illustrated book of which I read every side bar, caption, and fine print. I discovered the author was the curator of Anthropology at the Museum of Natural History that I had been visiting. In one of my classically bold and impulsive moments, I picked up the phone and called the museum, asking to speak with him. To my surprise, they put me through to his extension, and he answered. Thinking fast on my feet, I told him I was interested in his field and asked if I could set up an interview with him. He accepted, and we made an appointment to meet in his office at the museum a few weeks later. I showed up at the museum, and they literally gave me a pass that said "VIP." I prepared 25 questions, which he was of course extremely enthusiastic about answering, as clearly this was what he cared about most. And then I was given a private tour guide who took me through all the archives rooms in the museum. It was amazing to see people restoring tapestries, sorting archeological finds.

Never be afraid to ask for a private interview. People most times are highly flattered and enthusiastic to share with you. Put yourself around those you want to be like and those who are living a dream similar to yours. Get their mentorship.

3. Listen for the Hook

The hook is the most recognizable phrase that stands out and is easily remembered in a song. It hooks the listener. It is the part of the song that everyone knows and can't get out of their head. Like, "All You Need is Love " (The Beatles), "She's buying a stairway to Heaven" (Led Zeppelin), or "Hello from the other side" (Adele), it often carries the core message of the song.

What is your hook or core message, the unique wisdom you have to share? What might you see or recognize about the world that others may not? What insights do you have to share related to what matters to you most?

It took years for me to clearly distill my hook, but hopefully I have clearly imparted it to you by now—We need you.

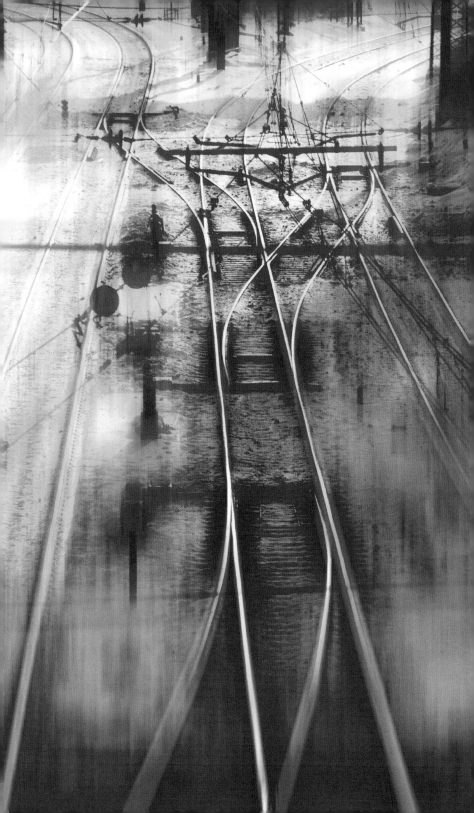

4. Edit & Delete as Needed

When you write and record songs, you write a lot more than you will ever share. You go down pathways and then find you need or want to abort mission. You edit tracks again and again and you delete others. You scrap what you once thought were your most brilliant lyrics.

One of the most important things I have learned to claim is my own right to change direction as needed, at will, and with utter authority. This may elicit skepticism and criticism from others, but it is essential and inevitable in bringing forth your true note. Accept that you must disappoint people. You are fluid, you are dynamic, and you are in charge. Your north star, your most reliable navigation tool, resides within your own chest. Every life journey is trial and error. Do not deny yourself the right to mess up, fall down, start again, or simply change your mind. All of these things are necessary and provide you with valuable feedback.

5. Create the Mix

Remember, our fundamental purpose is to illuminate the greater net. We are here to light our part of the overall web. How does your role correspond to the world outside of you? Where are you needed? How can you share your wisdom and your medicine? Who are your collaborators close by in your neighborhood of the net? Find who you can work in conjunction with. Find those whose mission supports yours and vice-versa. Dreaming a world is a collaborative effort. Creating the mix makes your song fuller. Like harmony, it adds color to your fundamental tone and a reverberating depth.

6. Master

A master is an authority in her field, someone one who masters her own life by living with integrity what she teaches. She has a revolving principle around which she lives, the distillation of what matters to her most. She holds the worldview, the big vision, not shying away from owning her medicine or her authority, but she is also not lost in her ego. A master recognizes she is one small but vital note in the collective chorus.

When you record a song, the master is the final product in which you make all your finishing touches, carefully balancing the frequencies and maximizing the loudness without losing the dynamics. Swami Satchidananda, a spiritual master and yoga adept, reinforces the idea that "There is no point in digging a hundred shallow wells." He tells us to dig one well deep. Every human being has the potential for mastery. Every soul deeply yearns to contribute. It is the purpose behind your purpose, the mission behind your mission. It is your soul promise to deliver on. It is vital, it is joy, true security and the fulfillment of your dream.

The Imaginal
Life Creed

YEARS AGO, I WROTE THE FOLLOWING as my personal creed. I kept a copy in my journal, in my purse, by my bed. In the really hard times, I read it upon waking and going to sleep to remind myself of the bigger picture. It carried me through dizzying times. I have a tradition of sharing it at my New Year's Day events. Many people have told me they have adopted it as their own. Please use mine, if it speaks to you, or better yet, author your own.

The Imaginal Life Creed

I AM ALIVE for the purpose of serving my individual growth, as well as the growth of the whole.

My wholehearted participation and generosity of spirit in sharing my gifts is the promise my soul made in taking this life.

I give my highest regard to how I feel, honoring my emotions as the messengers from my source, that they truly are.

I resolve to live in alignment with my True Self.

I pledge to no longer abstain from self-love.

With my thoughts, I create my world. I aim to focus my attention on well being, rather than the absence of it.

I consider my highest achievement and my greatest success, to be a state of Joy.

My inner lover knows I am on a holy mission, a grand treasure hunt of finding out through what I love what I have come to offer.

Each inhale is an invitation from life, a call to union.

Each exhale is my reply, an acceptance of this invitation and an offering of my spirit.

Before opening my eyes each morning, I aspire to open my heart, awakening and inviting the inner lover to steward my life.

I offer my life, my existence, as a sacred meeting ground for Great Love, the blessed and precious union of Spirit and Matter.

Amy McTear

Acknowledgments

First and foremost, profound gratitude to my mother, whose belief in me even I found unreasonable at times. Your open-minded interest in my work and essential support enabled me to write this book.

Special gratitude to my coach and mentor, Jeffrey Davis, for helping me distill my message and for your gentle honesty and relentless high standards. Many thanks to graphic designer, Holly Moxley, for your patience and incredible artistic sensitivity in manifesting my inner vision. And, much gratitude to Jen Kiaba, for helping me feel comfortable in front of the camera.

Deep gratitude to my soul brother, Joseph Jastrab, who has been a sound board and mirror for me throughout the years. Heartfelt appreciation for my co-parent, Craig Weinstein, whose willingness to rewrite how we parent and partner freed me to offer my most valuable gifts. And, loving thanks to my partner, Michael Ponte, whose quiet strength and extraordinary presence in my heart and home, gave me what I needed each day to persist in bringing this book to fruition.

I would not have been able to write this book without the many clients over the years who awakened and inspired me through the sharing of their inner lives, or without the audiences who resounded their love, longing, grief and hope.

Lastly, a very deep bow to the many children, teens and young adults I have worked with over the years, whose reflections of the world have motivated me to want to give all I can.

About the Author

Amy McTear is a motivational speaker, musician, mentor and spiritual activist who encourages people to live joyfully in tune with their true nature to create valuable, personally fulfilling lives. Her signature programs have touched thousands over the years, weaving voice, music, mindfulness, visual inspiration, eclectic instrumentation and community song in a way that helps audiences disarm, bond, become more self-aware and motivated to improve their lives and contribute to a more harmonious world.

www.AmyMcTear.com